ॐ

Oslo Paris Bern
TRAVELOGUE

Innocence Beauty Perfection
NATURALLY MANMADE

Ashwini Kumar Aggarwal

जय गुरुदेव

ISBN13: 978-93-48012-00-5 Paperback Edition
ISBN13: 978-93-48012-10-4 Hardbound Edition
ISBN13: 978-93-48012-56-2 Digital Edition

Title: **Oslo Paris Bern Travelogue**
Author: **Ashwini Kumar Aggarwal**

Printed and Published by
Devotees of Sri Sri Ravi Shankar Ashram
34 Sunny Enclave, Devigarh Road,
Patiala 147001, Punjab, Bhārat

https://advaita56.in/ The Art of Living Centre
https://www.artofliving.org/

Devotees Library Cataloging-in-Publication Data
Aggarwal, Ashwini Kumar.
Language: English. Thema: WTM WJ 2A 5H 6CA
BISAC: TRV010000 TRAVEL / Essays & Travelogues
Keywords: 1. Norway Innocence. 2. France Beauty. 3 Switzerland Perfection
Typeset in 12 Segoe UI

14th September 2025 Sunday, Back home feels good, cozy, natural. Ready for big great galactic works! Ashwin Masa, Krishna Paksha Ashtami Tithi, Rohini Nakshatra, Sharad Ritu, Dakshinayana.

Vikram Samvat 2082 Kalayukta, Saka Era 1947 Vishvavasu

1st Edition September 2025

जय गुरुदेव

Dedication

Sri Sri Ravi Shankar

who taught us to honor, revere, respect all

Acknowledgements

Sunview Harmony project best in class 97 acre township.

Blessing

Guru tattva is the principal, the wisdom. Guru is a tattva – an element, a quality inside you. It is not limited to a body or a form. Life and the Guru are inseparable.

Sri Sri Ravi Shankar
Navratri, Bangalore Ashram 13 Oct 2012

Prayer

oṃ asato mā sad gamaya I tamaso mā jyotir gamaya I
mṛtyor mā amṛtaṃ gamaya I oṃ śāntiḥ śāntiḥ śāntiḥ II
O Loving Divine!
Lead us from the shakiness to the firmness.
Lead us from the ignorance to the wisdom.
Lead us from the transient to the eternal.
Peace in our heart, in our body, and in our environs.

Prologue

Prepared documents for visa. Spent a month to get visa appointment date. https://visa.vfsglobal.com/ind/en/nor/apply-visa

- Schengen travel medical insurance taken for €30,000
- Visa processing fee to embassy paid €90
- Visa service charges to VFS paid €8
- Travel dates given, Invite letter submitted
- Hotel reservation submitted
- Upon arrival in Schengen, return ticket to be shown

We got it for 29th July 2025. VFS Global office, adjacent Elante Mall, Chandigarh. Reached on time for the 11:45am slot and were ushered in for application documents checking. Noticed incorrect place of birth, well O well! Got the photo clicked, then went for bio-metrics to another room and there also a photo was taken. Finally they took the passport and put all our application documents in a courier envelope and sealed it. Paid VFS Rs 400 cash for passport delivery charges.

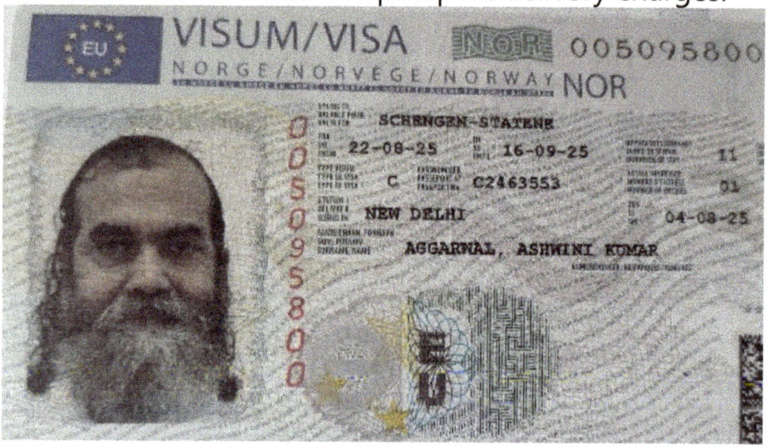

Passport received with visa stamping on 6th Aug by courier. Visa dated 4/8/2025. Visa duration 26 days, stay validity 11 days, single entry.

Contents

Amritsar Airport drive

It happened quickly. AT 7pm DURING DRIVE WE GOT CLU FOR SUNVIEW HARMONY. Drive became magical. Tour had already reset to the graceful. Well begun is half done. Ye!

Amritsar Doha Oslo

- Qatar boeing dreamliner Flight Amritsar to Doha
- Qatar boeing dreamliner Flight Doha to Oslo

Plane taxiing at Doha airport upon landing

Hamad International Airport, Doha, Qatar

Good news is Rare yet it heals in-toto.

Travel Summary

Traveler: Ashwini Kumar Aggarwal, Jagjit Singh Grewal

Date	Dep. Time	From	To	Flight No	Terminal	Airline Name
06SEP	0335	AMRITSAR ATQ	DOHA DOH	QR549		QATAR AIRWAYS
06SEP	0835	DOHA DOH	OSLO OSL	QR175		QATAR AIRWAYS
13SEP	0940	ZURICH ZRH	DOHA DOH	QR094		QATAR AIRWAYS
13SEP	1955	DOHA DOH	AMRITSAR ATQ	QR548		QATAR AIRWAYS

Business Class
QATAR
Boarding Pass
ASHWINI KUMAR AGGARWAL
0835
06SEP DOH-OSL
Boarding 0750
Seat 3K
Flight QR 175
SEQ-129
YOU ARE INVITED TO DEP AL MOURJAN
BUSINESS CLASS
ASHWINI KUMAR AGGARWAL
DOH-OSL
3K
QR175 06SEP
ETKT 1572790284545-2
PCS: 2 CKWT: 28 UNCKWT: SEQ NO: 129

Cycling is common all over Europe

Oslo

Norway believes in Innocence...

Norsk Troll

Losby Gods - Golfclub

20 min drive from Oslo, our first halt in Norway.
Losby Golfklubb
Losbyveien 270, 1475 Finstadjordet, Norway
Phone: +47 67 92 33 00, reservations@losbygods.no

Unmatched calmness, innocence. Golf Club.

Sprawling golf lawns and a laden apple tree greeted us.

Our stay at Losby Gods hotel, established 1850.

A Norsk Wedding

There was a wedding happening just as we entered Losby Gods, in the beautiful scenic setting. Girls and Women in Bunad, the traditional Norwegian dress graced the occasion.

A painting by Swedish painter Carl Larsson 1917.

Fjellhamar - Friendly Family Welcome

Daljit and Pawan the friendly couple seeing us off at Oslo Airport. Visitors here walk right upto auto-baggage-check-in! 8:43am 8th Sep 2025. I visited our Norsk family's home on 7th Sept in Fjellhamar, 20 min drive from Oslo.

Fjellhamar Skole the largest primary school in Norway.

Daljit Ashwini Pawanpreet – Arrival Oslo Airport 2pm 6th Sep

Holmenkollen - Ski Jump

7pm 6th Sep, a walk from parking lot to Holmenkollen

Architect: Julien De Smedt http://jdsa.eu/hop/ redone in 2011. Originally opened 1892.

The mind perishes. The body and soul remain.
Physics has stability. Chemistry is volatile.

A
B
TOUGHEST

Aker Brygge - Oslo Downtown

Oslo. Aker Brygge harbor.

Oslo Town Hall, Aker Brygge

8pm Opera had just ended, happy chatting people came out.

Nobel Peace Prize Award Center, Olso

You can do the practices. You can follow the Master. You can have discipline and good conduct. But being centered is difficult. Very very difficult.

Watch a show. Sing and clap. Jive mebbe.
Be with HAPPY people of ALL age groups.

Drøbak & Oscarsborg Fortress

2pm 7th Sep. Drive from Oslo to Drøbak
Tourist Information Center, Havnegata 4, 1440 Drøbak
+47 481 08 992. Sea view from jetty.

A passing Colorline Cruise Ship-Oslo Norway to Kiel Denmark.

Drøbak beach, view of Oscarsborg island in the distance.

Our Ferry from Drøbak to Oscarsborg island.

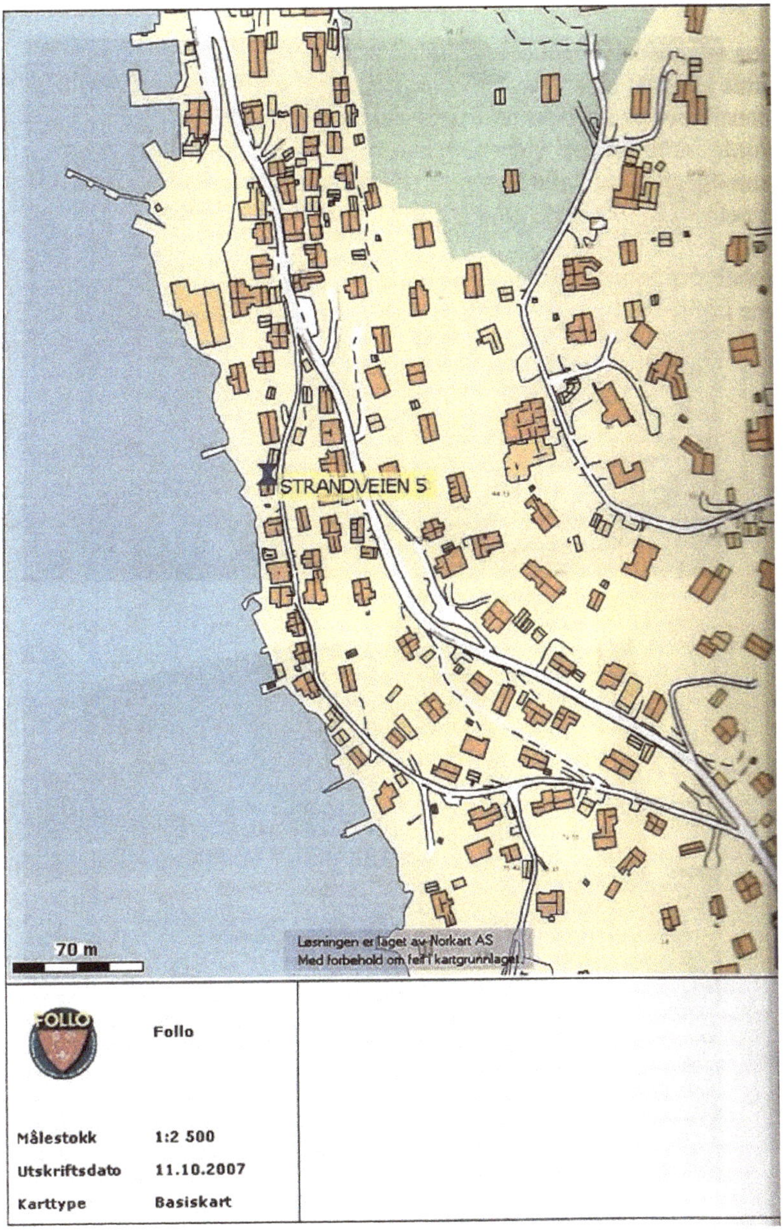

Drobak hand drawn map from 2007.

Anchor and Drøbak. There is a one-to-one relation.

Canon at Oscarsborg fortress. Used in 1940 WWII.

Closeup of a torpedo. Used in 1940 WWII. Oscarsborg Fortress (*norsk Oscarsborg Festning*) is named after King Oscar I of Sweden and Norway.

Oscarsborg fortress is 5min via tourist ferry from Drøbak.

Ferries anchored at the fortress

100th anniversary plaque at Oscarsborg Fortress
By Arnstein Rønning - Own work, CC BY-SA 3.0,
https://commons.wikimedia.org/w/index.php?curid=26824280

Vigeland Park

Angry Boy (*Sinna Taggen*)

Frogner Sculpture Park by Gustav Vigeland, Oslo

You can get pleasures. You can get powers.
Siddhis. Wealths. Resources.
Fame and anything else that is coveted.

However being **centered** is something else.
It is not easy. It is really hard to become centered.

Paris

France practices Beauty...

Arrived at Golden Tulip hotel located 7km from airport.

Room 512

SAS craft Oslo to Paris

Paris Airport

Maison&Objet

Décor and Design Trade Fair, an unsatisfying visit.
https://www.maison-objet.com/en/paris/visit

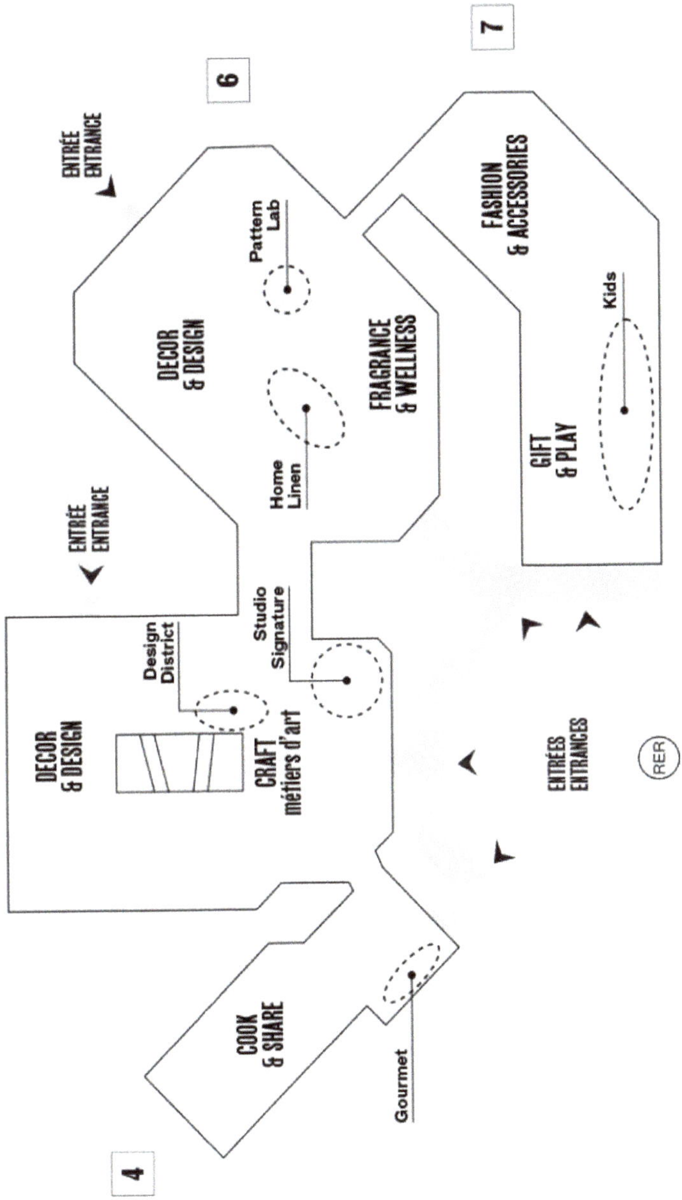

Lamps we liked, exchanging business card with the creator

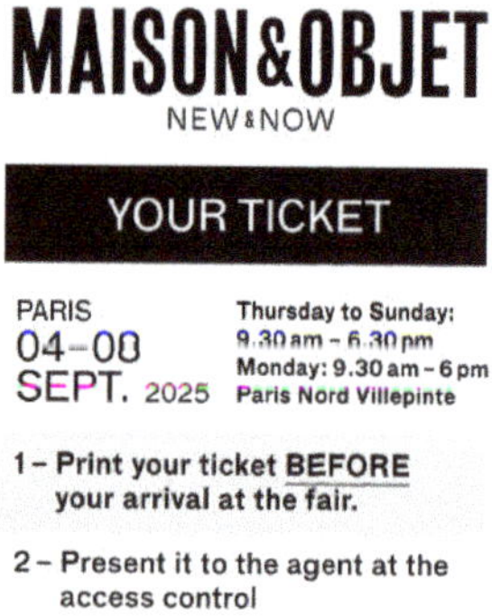

Self-standing floor lamps with soothing light

POLDR
DESIGN
HALL 5A
B 56
DECOR
& DESIGN

THE KIOSK
MAISON
&OBJET

dining dash of color

temp controlled garden hut

Roissy en France

Our cab for outing was 2 hours late, so we walked over to the L'Orangerie Cultural Center located on Allée du Verger, 95700 Roissy. There we saw the landing gear of a Concorde aircraft and its scupture in foil.

foil sculpture of concorde

illustration from Musée de l'Air et de l'Espace, Le Bourget. Paris

https://www.tripadvisor.com/Tourism-g196587-Roissy_en_France_Val_d_Oise_Ile_de_France-Vacations.html

landing gear of a crashed jet – weight 3ton *(Train d'Atterissage du Concorde)*

CONCORDE

MAIN LANDING GEAR

WEIGHT OF LANDING GEAR : 3,455 KG
TOTAL HEIGHT UP TO WING ATTACHMENT: 4.70 M
LOAD BEARING CAPACITY : 23,137 KG PER WHEEL
SHOCK STRUT EXTENSION : 46.5 CM. THE SHOCK STRUTS RETRACT THE LANDING GEAR INTO THE WINGS ON TAKE-OFF
BRAKE PRESSURE : 1,200 PSI

Serial number : F-BVFF

PARIS-RIO DE
27 ANNÉES DE
E COMMERCIALE
ELIANT PARIS À
IT NOTAMMENT
J BOURGET. CES
IOIRES DE TOUS

CONCORDE MADE ITS FIRST PASSENGER FLIGHT FROM PARIS TO RIO DE JANEIRO VIA DAKAR ON 21ST JANUARY 1976. AFTER 27 YEARS OF LOYAL SERVICES RENDERED, THIS LEGENDARY AIRCRAFT WAS RETIRED IN JUNE 2003, FOLLOWING ITS LAST FLIGHT FROM PARIS TO NEW YORK. NOWADAYS, THE AIRCRAFT CAN BE ADMIRED IN VARIOUS MUSEUMS, AMONGST WHICH THE AIR AND SPACE MUSEUM IN LE BOURGET NEAR PARIS, THUS KEEPING THE MEMORY OF CONCORDE ALIVE FOREVER.

CONCORDE'S TECHNICAL FEATURES

WINGSPAN : 25.56 M - HEIGHT TO TOP OF TAILFIN : 12.21 M
WING SURFACE : 358.25 SQ. M - LENGTH : 62.19 M
WEIGHT : 78.7 METRIC TONS EMPTY. MAXIMUM TAKE-OFF WEIGHT : 185.1 METRIC TONS FULLY LOADED (FUEL AND PASSENGERS)
MAXIMUM CRUISING SPEED : MACH 2.02 (2,146 KM/HR)
CRUISING ALTITUDE : 18,288 M
MAXIMUM RANGE : 6,100 KM (WITH 100 PASSENGERS)
PROPULSION : 4 ROLLS-ROYCE OLYMPUS 593 MK 610 ENGINES:
ENGINE THRUST : 17,260 KG WITH POST COMBUSTION ON TAKE-OFF

Roissy
CLÉ DE FRANCE
OFFICE DE TOURISME - TOURISM OFFICE
ROISSY-EN-FRANCE

THIS PART WAS KINDLY OFFERED BY AIR FRANCE TO THE TOWN OF ROISSY-EN-FRANCE ON THE RETIREMENT OF THE CONCORDE IN JUNE 2003.

CLASSÉE STATION DE TOURISME

ROISSY-EN-FRANCE
NOS COUPS DE CŒUR À ROISSY-EN-FRANCE
OUR FAVOURITES IN ROISSY-EN-FRANCE
SE BALADER / GOING FOR A WALK
AUTOROUTE DU NORD
CENTRE COMMERCIAL AÉROVILLE
GOLF INTERNATIONAL DE ROISSY
WHERE TO EAT

Local town hall

Local traditional restaurent

La Vallée Village

Excitedly we made our Paris start with a visit to the shopping street that has inspired Sunview Plaza in Ludhiana.

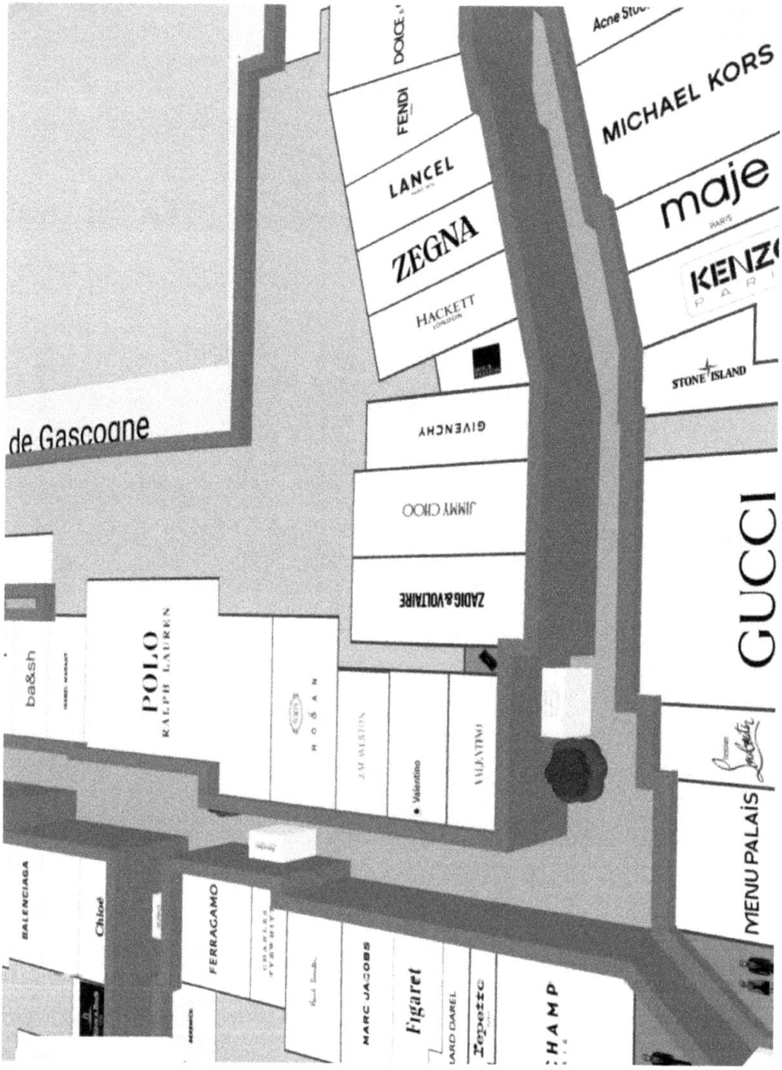

LA VALLÉE
VILLAGE

Chloé

LONGCHAMP
PARIS

La Vallée skyline is gorgeous

la femme de **La Vallée Village**, stone's throw from Paris.

I am just a traveler. A stranger in **RED BOOTS**

Sitting quietly…hopeful!

Louis Vuitton Champs-Élysées.

La Défense Business District

Facing page - The Esplanade at La Défense.

posing at the Thumb...Man's sign of solidarity.

'Le Pouce,' a 40-foot high thumb sculpture by César Baldaccini, 1965.

Slim electric scooters for a single-person-standing-ride were popular all over where we visited in Europe.

People simply hired them using Voi, Ryde, and Bolt apps and dropped them when their ride was finished, (to work or shop or play, whereever. It was left right there. The next person who wished to hire it was alerted for any nearby Scooties...all unmanned, convenient and "safe" for within city movement.

Painting is Great! Trying one's hand at sketching

M
'O
Musée
d'Orsay

Gare et hôtel d'Orsay
architecte
Victor Laloux
(1898-1900)
Musée d'Orsay
architectes
ACT Architecture
Renaud Bardon
Pierre Colboc
Jean-Paul Philippon
(1979-1986)
Gae Aulenti
(1980-1986)

Pénélope in white marble by Jules Cavelier 1849

Eve avant le péché (woman before intercourse) in white marble by Eugene Delaplanche 1891

Auguste Rodin 1881 *Le Penseur* The Thinker, The Poet

royal antique chair

Pierre-Auguste Renoir, *Julie Manet, dit aussi l'Enfant au chat* 1887

Vincent Van Gogh, *Le restaurant de la Sirène à Asnières,*1887

Adolf Schreyer *Charge de l'artillerie de la Garde impériale à Traktir en Crimée* 1865

Vincent Van Gogh *La chambre de Van Gogh à Arles, 1889.*

Vincent Van Gogh *The Italian Woman – Agostina Segatori, 1887*

Cleopatra's Needle

The 74 feet tall Cleopatra's Needle located at the center of Place de la Concorde in Paris is originally Egypt's Obelisk of Luxor, an ancient 3200 year old monument carved from pink granite by Emperor Ramesses II. It found its way to Paris in 1836. A glittering 12 feet pyramidion on its top made of bronze and 23.5 carat gold leaf, was installed in 1998.

Three of the four original obelisks were moved to Alexandria and set up in the Caesarium, a temple built by Queen Cleopatra in honor of Mark Antony, thus these got named Cleopatra's needles.

Original site of the Paris obelisk, its twin is still in Luxor Egypt.

Inscription diagrams show how the Oelisk was lowered in Egypt and raised in Paris.

Cleopatra's Needle - the Obelisk from Luxor Egypt.

Eiffel Tower

View from Pont d'Iéna bridge side, overlooking the Seine river.
We arrived at 6:50pm 9th Sept.

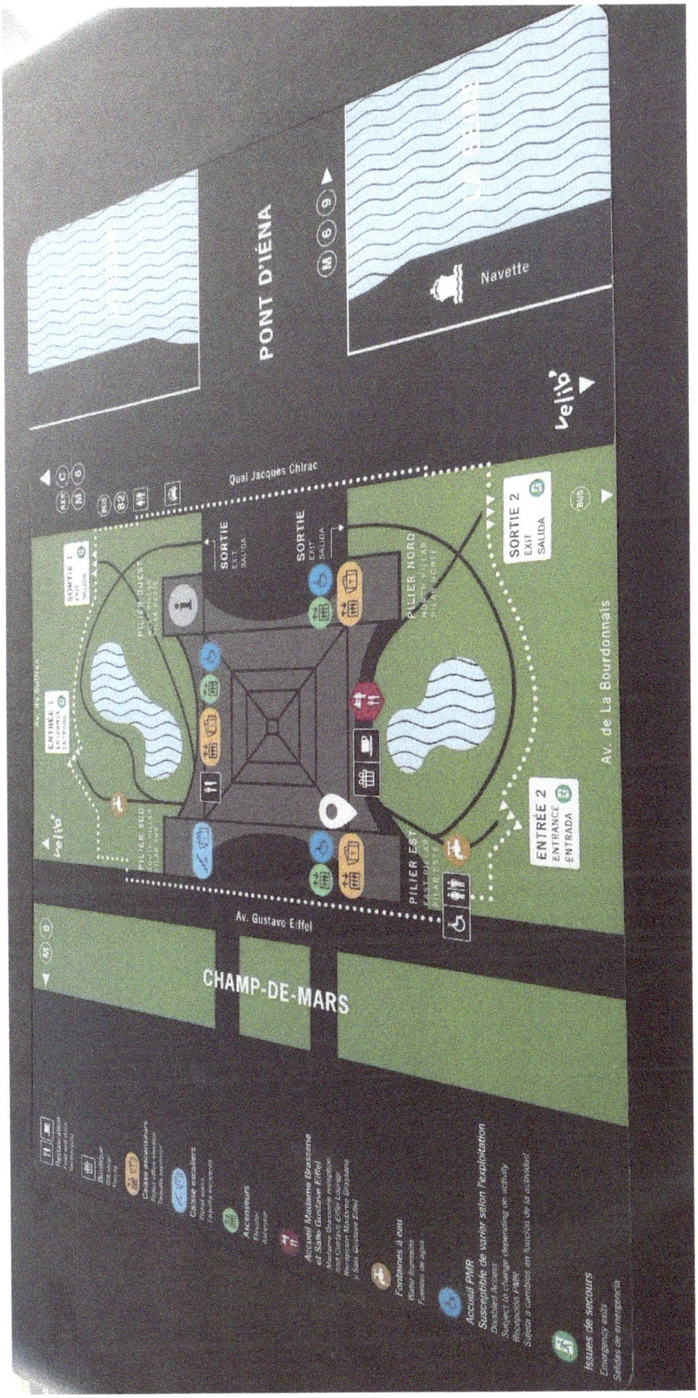
PONT D'IÉNA
Navette
Quai Jacques Chirac
SORTIE
EXIT
SALIDA
SORTIE 1
SORTIE 2
ENTRÉE 1
ENTRÉE 2
ENTRANCE
ENTRADA
PILIER OUEST
PILIER NORD
PILIER SUD
PILIER EST
Av. de La Bourdonnais
Av. Gustave Eiffel
CHAMP-DE-MARS
Accueil Madame Brassens et Salle Gustave Eiffel
Ascenseurs
Caisse escaliers
Fontaines à eau
Accueil PMR
Susceptible de varier selon l'exploitation
Issues de secours
Emergency exits
Salidas de emergencia

View from ticket queue, close up of iron structure.

Paris from Eiffel Tower top

Ici le 25 Août 1944
aux ordres du Capitaine SARNIGUET,
les sergents Henri DURIAUX, Pierre NOËL,
le caporal Charles ROUARD,
les sapeurs Marcel CONVERSY, André TAILLEFER,
du Régiment de Sapeurs-Pompiers de PARIS
ont hissé le drapeau tricolore
dans la capitale encore occupée.

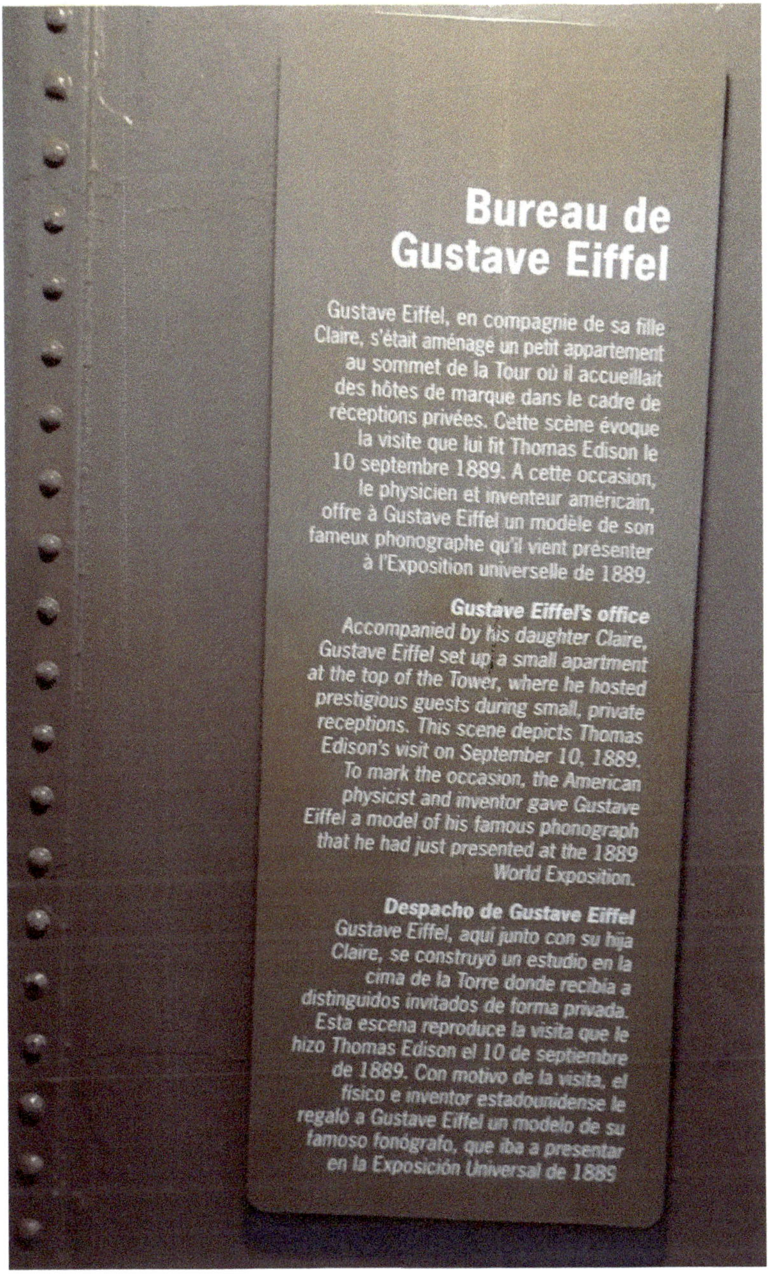
Bureau de
Gustave Eiffel
Gustave Eiffel, en compagnie de sa fille Claire, s'était aménagé un petit appartement au sommet de la Tour où il accueillait des hôtes de marque dans le cadre de réceptions privées. Cette scène évoque la visite que lui fit Thomas Edison le 10 septembre 1889. A cette occasion, le physicien et inventeur américain, offre à Gustave Eiffel un modèle de son fameux phonographe qu'il vient présenter à l'Exposition universelle de 1889.
Gustave Eiffel's office
Accompanied by his daughter Claire, Gustave Eiffel set up a small apartment at the top of the Tower, where he hosted prestigious guests during small, private receptions. This scene depicts Thomas Edison's visit on September 10, 1889. To mark the occasion, the American physicist and inventor gave Gustave Eiffel a model of his famous phonograph that he had just presented at the 1889 World Exposition.
Despacho de Gustave Eiffel
Gustave Eiffel, aquí junto con su hija Claire, se construyó un estudio en la cima de la Torre donde recibía a distinguidos invitados de forma privada. Esta escena reproduce la visita que le hizo Thomas Edison el 10 de septiembre de 1889. Con motivo de la visita, el físico e inventor estadounidense le regaló a Gustave Eiffel un modelo de su famoso fonógrafo, que iba a presentar en la Exposición Universal de 1889

We left at 8:50pm 9th Sep.

One day you shall have to transcend Time, nay Space.

Get out of the domain of planet Earth.
Get out of the cycle of life and death.

Drop the patterns.
Drop the repetitions.

Neutralize the notions,
assumptions,
concepts,
conclusions.

Switzerland

Switzerland lives in Perfection...

Basel

Took SAS flight from Paris France to EuroAirport Basel Mulhouse Freiburg Switzerland. EuroAirport serves three adjacent cities, Basel in Switzerland, Mulhouse in France, and Freiburg in Germany, hence the name.

Basel
Muttenz
Sissach
Liestal
BASEL LANDSCHAFT
Laufen
Breitenbach
Waldenburg
Frick
Brugg
Baden
Dielsdorf
Wettingen
Aarau
Lenzburg
Zürich
Olten
Aarburg
SOLOTHURN
Moutier
Niederbipp
Oensingen
Aare
Zofingen
Unterkulm
Bremgarten
Reuss
Muri
Affoltern
Reinach
Solothurn
Grenchen
Wangen
Langenthal
Dagmersellen
Herzogenbuchsee
Sursee
Sempacher See
Sempach
Hochdorf
Cham
Zuger See
Büren
Huttwil
Willisau
Emmenbrücke
Küssnacht
Fraubrunnen
Luzern
LUZERN
Burgdorf
Hasle
Kriens
Vierwaldstätter See
BERNE
Bolligen
Entlebuch
Emmental
Langnau
Schüpfheim
Stans
Worb
Köniz
Schlosswil
Sarnen
NIDWALDEN
Belp
Münsingen
OBWALDEN
Marbach
Giswil
Schwarzenburg
Engelberg
Wattenwil
Thun
BERN
Brienz
Titlis
Brienzer See
Thuner See
Meiringen
Innertkirchen
Spiez
Interlaken
Schwarzhorn
Wimmis
Dammastock
Grindelwald
Gotthardtunnel
Lauterbrunnen

Bern

Perfect cobblestone footpaths.

Clocks and watches with legendary Swiss accuracy.

Swiss Parliament. CURIA CONFOEDERATIONIS HELVETICAE

Bundesplatz (Federal Square), Bern. Opposite the Parliament. Relish the smooth lines, clean paint, and the classy *new* look of each building.

Swiss National Bank at Bundesplatz. Adjacent is the Parliament.

Tram

Tram line

Fashionable doorway

BERCHTOLDVS. V DVX. ZAERING.
RECT. BVRGVND. VRBIS. CONDITOR.
TVRRIM. ET. PORTAM. FECIT.
A. CHRI. MCXCI.
EA. RENOVATA. MDCCLXX.

20
Neuengasse 20
BRIGITTE GASSER
URFER TREUHAND AG
Akupunktur Ch. Bürgi
Craniosacraltherapie D. Studer
Mondo AG Mondo Bene AG
IAF Romandie & Ticino
Premium Consulting GmbH
andor holding AG
globetrotter
Explore Events
Osteopathie
Rachèle Monnier
swiss safelab
KMU Stadt Bern
GEWERBE TREUHAND AG BERN

Interlaken (Brienz lake)

Enjoying a walk in the town Interlaken nestled between two crystal clear blue lakes. Bridge across Brienz lake.

Car drive Interlaken to Grindelwald, perfect Swiss landscapes

Congress_Kursaal Interlaken

Walking promenade

Grindelwald

Best place to stay and hike, enjoy farm-fresh Swiss milk and cheese and honey. We spent two nights, hiking and soaking in Swiss delights, from 6:30pm 10th Sep to 11:30am 12th Sep. It snowed on 10th and 11th nights on the peaks, increasing the beauty.

The friendly unattended farm shops everywhere in Switzerland. With a fridge from where you may take milk, cheese, honey and leave money by yourself. (empty plastic milk bottles also provided so you can fill as much as you want).

GrindelwaldBus
Kirche
Grindelwald
121 Oberer Gletscher
122 Gletscherschlucht
124 Bodmi
nur Winter / winter only
128 Schwarzwaldalp
nur Sommer / summer only
GrindelwaldBus
Kirche
Kirche
Wetterhorn-Aufzug

Typical house elevation in Grindelwald

A coffee roastery

A small fountain, typical of Switzerland public places.

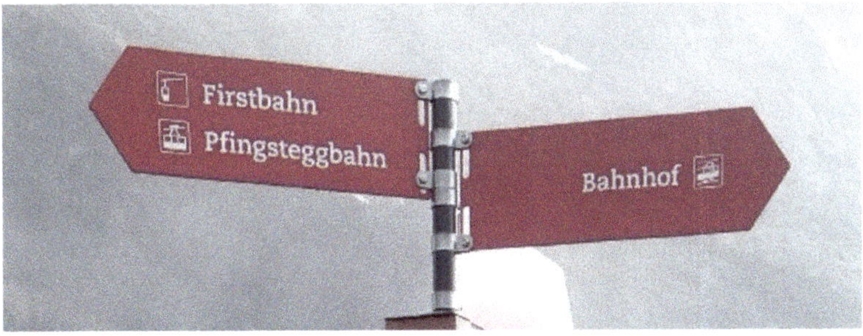

In Grindelwald I walked for 90 minutes from 9:30am to 11am on both days to the 2.8km point and back, on the hike trail. After a perfect stay at Grindelwald, we left for Lauterbrunnen waterfall. Then we visited the Aare river gorge. Spent time circling the deep blue Breinz lake, before moving to Lucerne, a very well made city. Then we drove to the old town Zürich, Rheinfall, and Jestetten, before returning to spend the night near Zürich airport.

Lauterbrunnen

Enjoyed a 20 min climb to Staubbachfall a high misty waterfall, midway on a cliff face. The return took 15 min and we felt extremely grateful.

Aareschlucht (Meiringen)

Traversed a 45 min walk along the *not so scary* Aare river gorge. A spectacular 1.4 km long natural wonder featuring a wooden walkway along the cliff face and also tunnels carved into the rock, between towering cliffs where the Aare river gushes through roaring loudly. Upon exit, we can take a local train back to the starting point, but we took our dhillon cab.

A well made park with a hanging pendulum wheel caught our attention at the Exit.

Lucerne

Luzern 4
Waid-Spital
Käferberg
Nordheim
Koblenz

7
Kapellplatz
JOSEPH WILLMANN-HAVS
HIER WOHNTEN
FRANZ VRS BALTHASAR
1689-1763
JOSEPH ANTON FELIX BALTHASAR
1737-1810
PATRIOTEN, STAATSMÄNNER,
GELEHRTE

ARCHÄOLOGIE
PARKHAUS OPÉRA

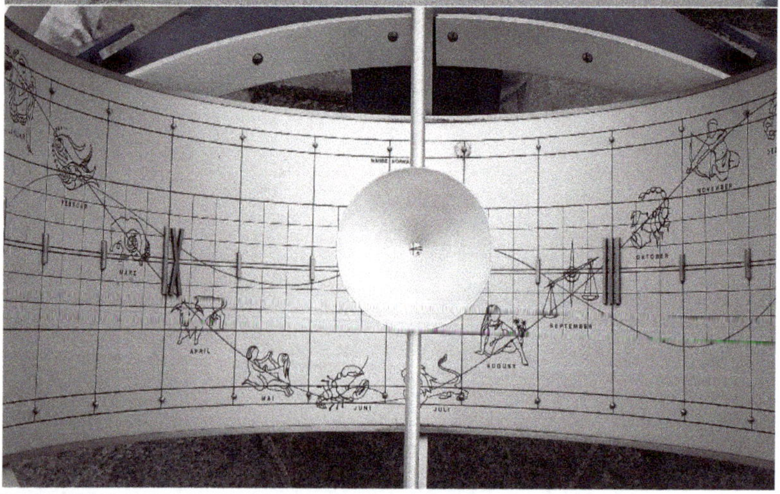
APRIL
MAI
JUNI
JULI
AUGUST
SEPTEMBER
OKTOBER

LUCERNE

UBS
UBS

WOHNIDEE Luzern - auf 8 Etagen

MAMMUT
FINALLY
HOME

Preis
Prix/Prezzo

12
Zahnarzt
Dr. Christian Büel
Dr. med. dent.
MARKUS BUEL
eidg. dipl. Zahnarzt
Physiotherapie
I.U. physio & coaching

Zürich

Stadelhoferplatz

7pm 12th Sep. A Ferrari at a parking lot in Zürich.

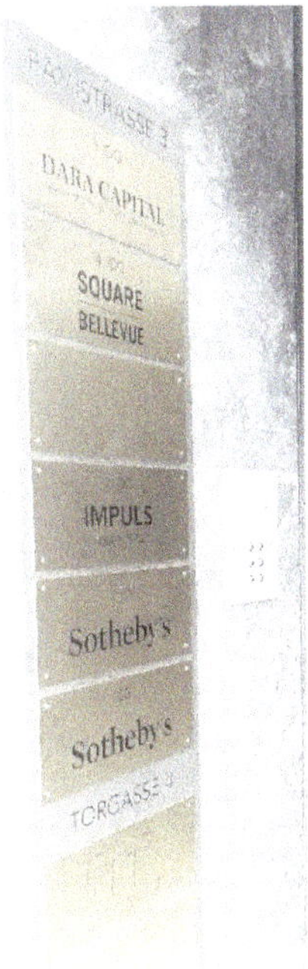

Sotheby's fine art gallery

Framed in a doorway. **storms** of **passions**

Even if you wish to play, for how long can you play? The same goes for rest and relaxation, soon you shall be up and about, and sooner you shall halt and rest.

Railway Station, Zürich

Galli
Galli
DOR
OMEGA
IWC
Galli
IWC

Rheinfall

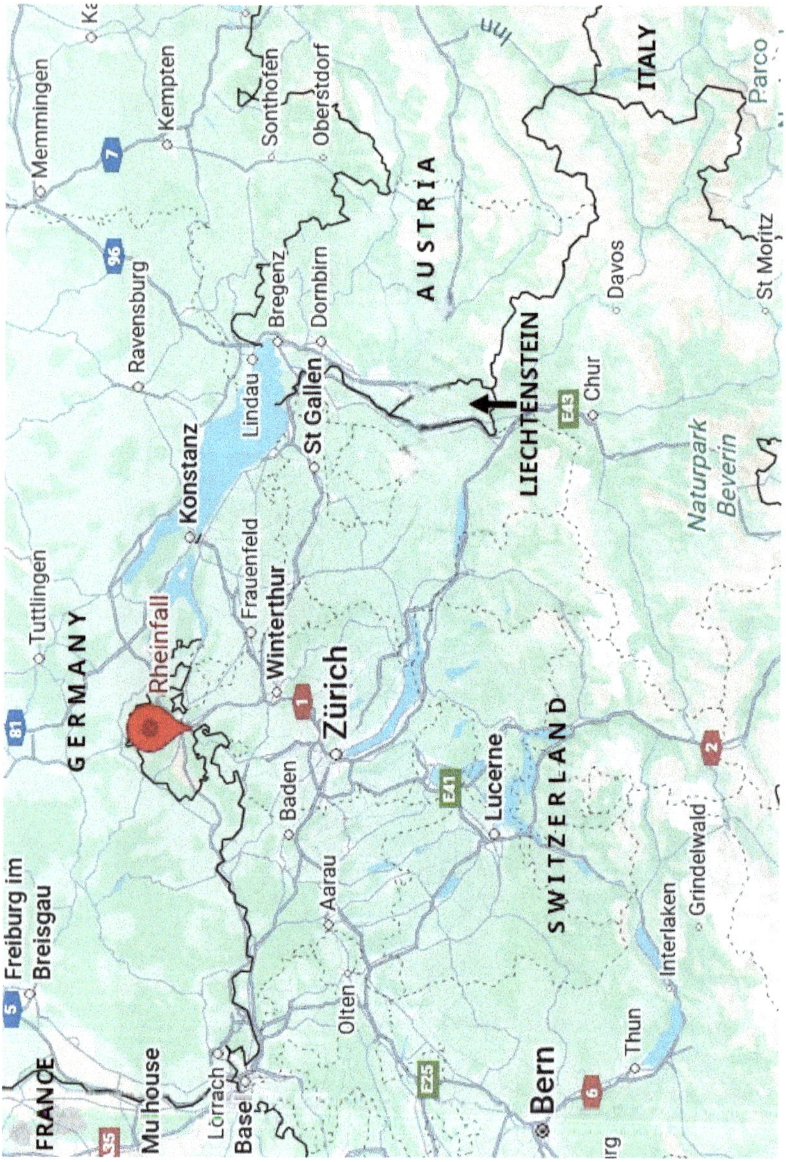
FRANCE
Mulhouse
Basel
Lörrach
Freiburg im Breisgau
GERMANY
Tuttlingen
Memmingen
Kempten
Ravensburg
Konstanz
Rheinfall
Frauenfeld
Winterthur
Zürich
Baden
Aarau
Olten
Bern
Thun
Interlaken
Grindelwald
SWITZERLAND
Lucerne
LIECHTENSTEIN
Chur
Davos
St Moritz
Naturpark Beverin
AUSTRIA
Lindau
Bregenz
Dornbirn
St Gallen
Sonthofen
Oberstdorf
Inn
ITALY
Parco
5
81
96
7
1
2
6
E25
E41
E43

Europe's largest waterfall by volume, located at address 8212 Neuhausen am Rheinfall, Switzerland

A smoke at the waterfall. THUNDER

a swiss letterbox

during car drive Rheinfall to Jestetten

German detour Jestetten

From Rheinfall, we drove across the border to Jestetten in Germany and stopped at Denns BioMarkt, a large grocery store to buy buns, cheese, fruits, juice and milk.

TAGESPREIS
Brombeeren
aus der Region
ca. 3,14
3,99

Take time Out

Regularly **sit** with Yourself. **Your** personal space is Beautiful. You shall be able to discriminate between the destructible and **in**destructible. This fine dividing thread starts **glowing**.

Going in a full **circle** you reach the beginning.
Going on a straight **line** you reach ... Anyways, these are just small games to excite the vibration, the **spanda**.

For sure i shall breakthrough it all. And be gone. I wish to go where Thought doesn't exist, where Sound and Sight have no role to play.

Read some Ancient texts

Once in a while **sit** at the feet of the Master. IGNITE YOUR MIND. OPEN YOUR HEART

Zürich Doha Amritsar flight

- Qatar boeing 787 dreamliner Flight Zürich to Doha
- Qatar boeing 320 Flight Doha to Amritsar

Qatar Airways		PNR	7JY9WR			Doha = -2:30 hours from India, Oslo = -3:30 hours			
Date	Flight	**Dep Local**	From	To	**Arr Local**	Flt Duration	Stopover	India Dep	India Arr
06,Sep	QR 549	**0335am**	Amritsar	Doha	**0505am**	4 hours	**3:30 hours**	0335am	0735am
06,Sep	QR 175	**0835am**	Doha	Oslo	**1430pm**	7 hours	-	1105am	1800pm
13,Sep	QR 094	**0940am**	Zurich	Doha	**1625pm**	5:45 hours	**3:30 hours**	1310pm	1905pm
13,Sep	QR 548	**1955pm**	Doha	Amritsar	**0210am**	3:45 hours	-	2225pm	0210am

Zürich airport boarding gate 8:53am 13th Sep return flight

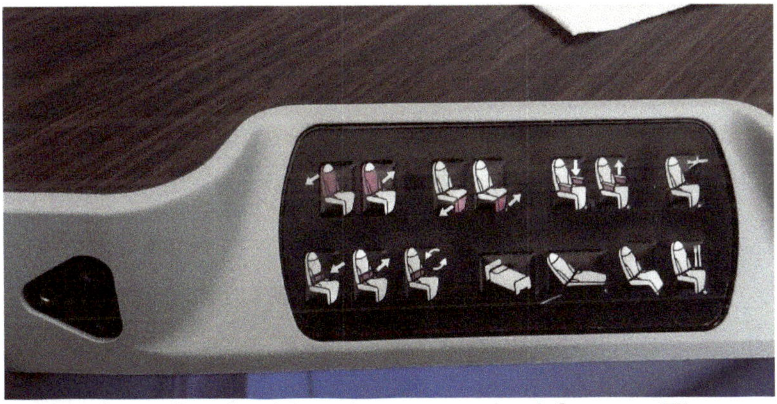
Boeing dreamliner business class seat-control-features. We can make it slide all the way to become just like a flat bed! We can make the armrests come up and down. We can have a gentle roller back massage.

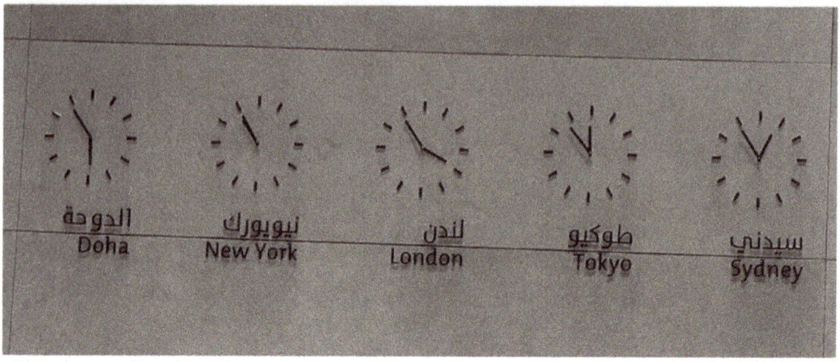

Clocks at Doha airport showing
5:54Doha 10:54NewYork 3:54London 11:54Tokyo 12:54Sydney

Technically as per time zone, the sequence is:
10:54am_New York 3:54pm_London 4:54pm_Paris
5:54pm_Doha 11:54pm_Tokyo 12:54am_next day_Sydney

Flights Hotels

Qatar Airlines – Amritsar to Oslo, and Zürich to Amritsar
Scandinavian Airlines – Oslo to Paris (Dep 10:45am Arr 1:10pm)
Air France – Paris to Basel (Dep 8:25am Arr 9:30am)

Oslo to Paris flight boarding pass

Charles-de-Gaulle airport Paris, waiting to board for Basel.

Oslo Losby Gods Room 254. Paris Golden Tulip Room 512

Grindelwald Sunstar Room 326. Zürich Radisson Room 116

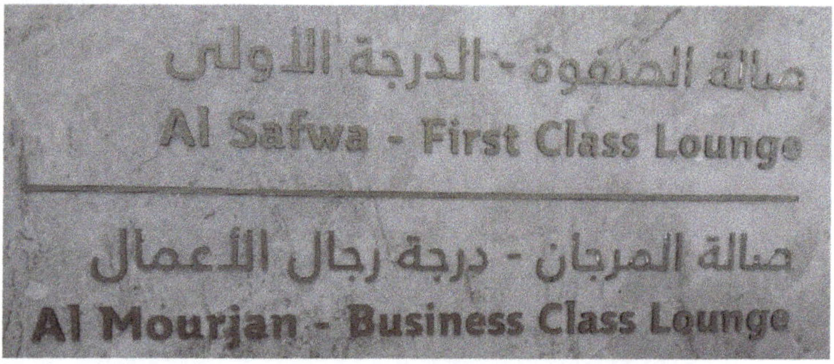

Doha Airport Lounge.

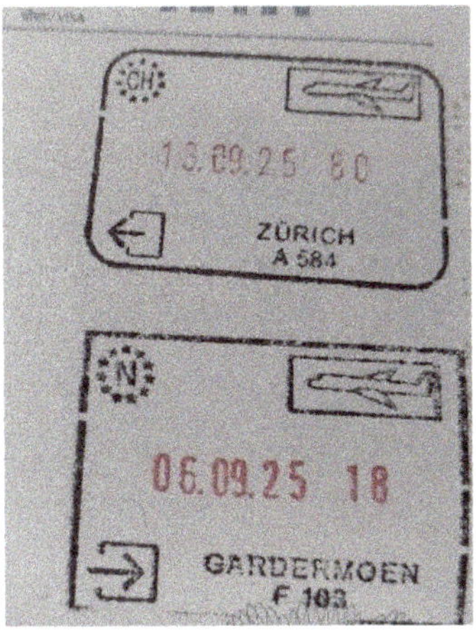

Zürich departure immigration stamp 13th Sep.
Oslo arrival immigration stamp 6th Sep.

India departure immigration stamp 6th Sep. Arrival stamp 14th Sep 2025.

Amritsar to home drive

All over quickly. Back to naturalness, cozy comforts. Potholes and fragrant incense...Havan and social chats.

India Departure 3:30am 6th September 2025.
India Arrival 2am 14th September 2025.

Delicacies

Fruits at Fjellhamar house. A bakery in Lucerne, Switzerland

Regaa, Paris offering Indian style foodstuffs. I had baked cauliflower and potato.

Samosa and Indian delicacies, Paris.

Banana and Tangerine. Nuts and Lime Juice

Midway halt during drive from Basel airport to Bern, Switzerland

Epilogue

At times Stop. Don't always Run.
Ponder hard on your Aim. Dance Clap. Sculpt Paint Sing.

सर्वे भवन्तु सुखिनः । सर्वे सन्तु निरामयाः ।
सर्वे भद्राणि पश्यन्तु । मा कश्चिद् दुःख भाग् भवेत् ॥
ॐ शान्तिः शान्तिः शान्तिः ॥

When faith has blossomed in life,
Every step is led by the Divine.

Sri Sri Ravi Shankar

Om Namah Shivaya

जय गुरुदेव

Imagine. Think. Dream. Innovate. Experiment. WorkHard.

www.ingramcontent.com/pod-product-compliance
Ingram Content Group UK Ltd.
Pitfield, Milton Keynes, MK11 3LW, UK
UKHW020051200726
13845UKWH00056B/802